W9-DFW-413

The European Union: key figures

Growing from six Member States in 1952 to 15 by 1995, the European Union today embraces more than 370 million people, from the Arctic Circle to Portugal, from Ireland to Crete. Though rich in diversity, the Member States share certain common values. By entering into partnership together, their aim is to promote democracy, peace, prosperity and a fairer distribution of wealth.

After establishing a true frontier-free Europe by eliminating the remaining barriers to trade among themselves, the Member States of the European Union have resolved to respond to the major economic and social challenges of the day — to establish a common currency, boost employment and strengthen Europe's role in world affairs. In so doing they will consolidate the foundations of a European Union that answers the needs of its citizens and is already preparing for further enlargement to include countries to the south and east.

This booklet contains a series of charts on the population of the Union and its Member States, their standard of living, employment, economy, Europe's place in the world, and the Union and its citizens. The charts, drawn up with the valuable help of Eurostat, the European Statistical Office, also show comparisons with the rest of the world and, in particular, with the Union's main partners and competitors. [1]

[1] The abbreviations used for the Union countries are shown on page 4.
USA = United States of America; JPN = Japan.
ECU 1 = approximately GBP 0.80, IEP 0.79 and USD 1.25 at exchange rates current on 1 October 1996.

1952 EUR 6

The European Community was originally founded by six States — Belgium, France, Germany, Italy, Luxembourg and the Netherlands — which were joined by Denmark, Ireland and the United Kingdom in 1973, Greece in 1981 and Spain and Portugal in 1986.
In 1990, the new east German *Länder* were incorporated.
In 1992, the Member States decided to form a European Union, which was enlarged in 1995 to include Austria, Finland and Sweden.

1973 EUR 9

1981 EUR 10

1986 EUR 12

1990 EUR 12

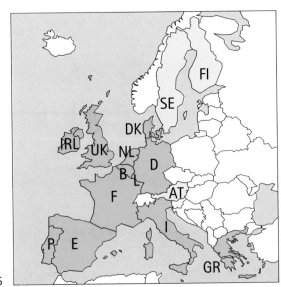

1995 EUR 15

Population

Area
Population size and density
Birth rates and life expectancy

Source: United Nations, *World Population Prospects*, 1994.

Population: a disturbing trend
Total population as a percentage of the world total

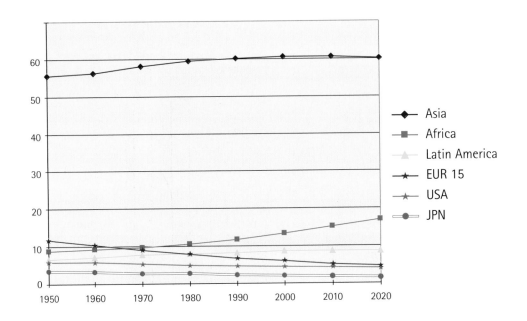

Source: Eurostat.

The European Union: relatively small in area
Area 1 000 km²

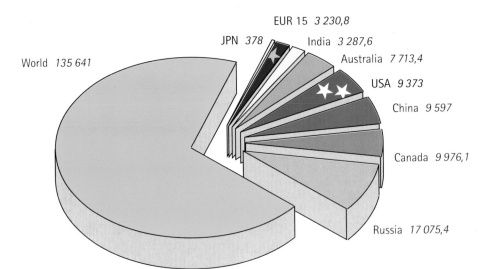

Source: Eurostat.

Population density: relatively high
Persons per km², 1995

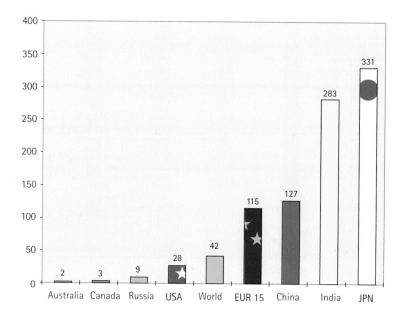

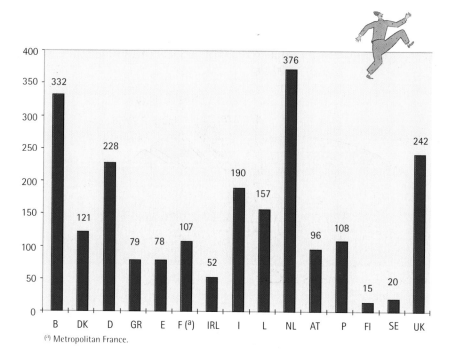

(ª) Metropolitan France.

Source: Eurostat.

Population: half as many young people as Africa
Population by age groups percentage, 1995

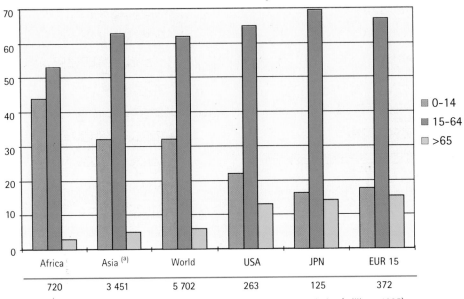

	Africa	Asia [a]	World	USA	JPN	EUR 15
	720	3 451	5 702	263	125	372

Total population (millions, 1995)

Legend: ■ 0-14   ■ 15-64   ▢ >65

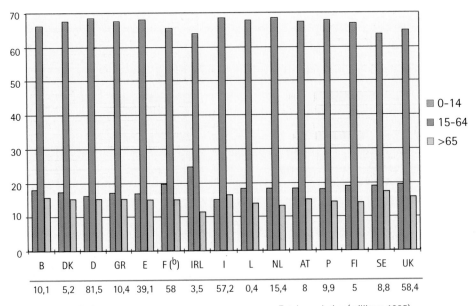

	B	DK	D	GR	E	F (b)	IRL	I	L	NL	AT	P	FI	SE	UK
	10,1	5,2	81,5	10,4	39,1	58	3,5	57,2	0,4	15,4	8	9,9	5	8,8	58,4

Total population (millions, 1995)

Legend: ■ 0-14   ■ 15-64   ▢ >65

(a) Including Turkey.
(b) Metropolitan France.

Sources: Eurostat, United Nations
World Population Prospects, 1994.

Birth rates: older generations not being replaced
Average number of children per woman

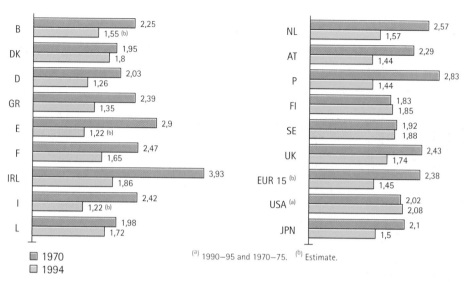

	1970	1994
B	2,25	1,55 (b)
DK	1,95	1,8
D	2,03	1,26
GR	2,39	1,35
E	2,9	1,22 (b)
F	2,47	1,65
IRL	3,93	1,86
I	2,42	1,22 (b)
L	1,98	1,72
NL	2,57	1,57
AT	2,29	1,44
P	2,83	1,44
FI	1,83	1,85
SE	1,92	1,88
UK	2,43	1,74
EUR 15 (b)	2,38	1,45
USA (a)	2,02	2,08
JPN	2,1	1,5

■ 1970
□ 1994

(a) 1990–95 and 1970–75.   (b) Estimate.

Life expectancy: a quarter of a century of progress
Life expectancy at birth (years)

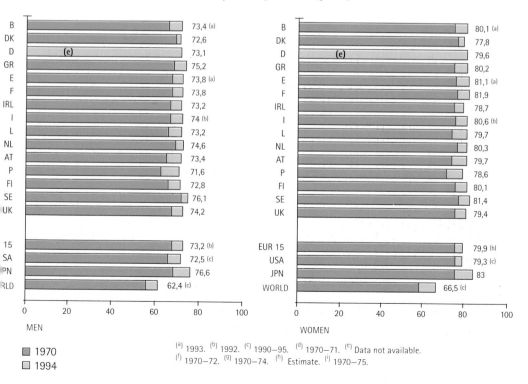

MEN

B	73,4 (a)
DK	72,6
D (e)	73,1
GR	75,2
E	73,8 (a)
F	73,8
IRL	73,2
I	74 (b)
L	73,2
NL	74,6
AT	73,4
P	71,6
FI	72,8
SE	76,1
UK	74,2
EUR 15	73,2 (b)
USA	72,5 (c)
JPN	76,6
WORLD	62,4 (c)

WOMEN

B	80,1 (a)
DK	77,8
D (e)	79,6
GR	80,2
E	81,1 (a)
F	81,9
IRL	78,7
I	80,6 (b)
L	79,7
NL	80,3
AT	79,7
P	78,6
FI	80,1
SE	81,4
UK	79,4
EUR 15	79,9 (b)
USA	79,3 (c)
JPN	83
WORLD	66,5 (c)

■ 1970
□ 1994

(a) 1993. (b) 1992. (c) 1990–95. (d) 1970–71. (e) Data not available.
(f) 1970–72. (g) 1970–74. (h) Estimate. (i) 1970–75.

Standard of living

Gross domestic product per head
Household consumption
Social security
Private equipment

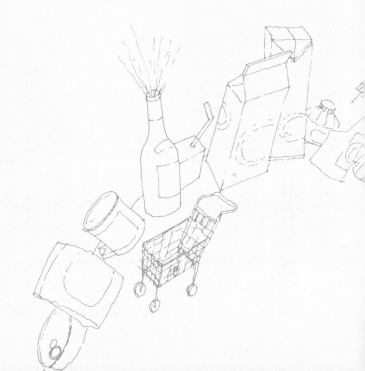

Source: Eurostat.

Gross domestic product: relatively prosperous ...
Gross domestic product (GDP) per head (in terms of purchasing power standards, [a] 1992)

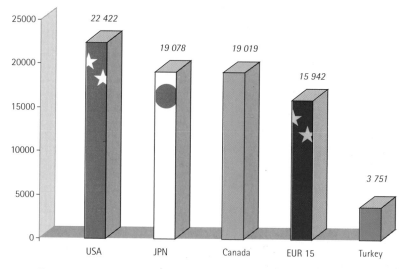

[a] These represent an identical volume of goods and services everywhere, irrespective of price levels.

GDP per head (in terms of purchasing power standards, 1994)

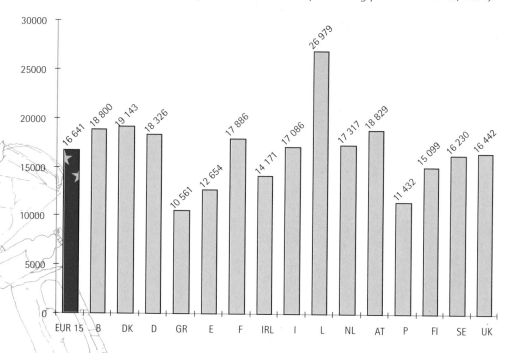

Source: Eurostat.

... but marked regional disparities

GDP per head in regions of the Union (in terms of purchasing power standards, 1993, EUR 15 = 100)

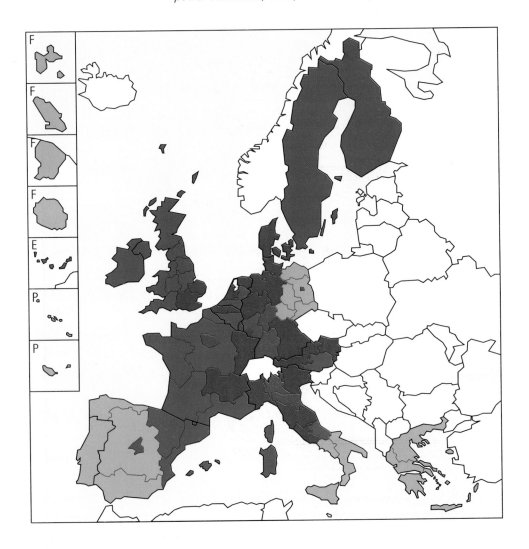

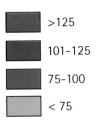

▓	>125
▓	101–125
▓	75–100
▓	< 75

Source: Eurostat.

Consumer spending: uneven growth
Household consumption per head (in constant ECU)

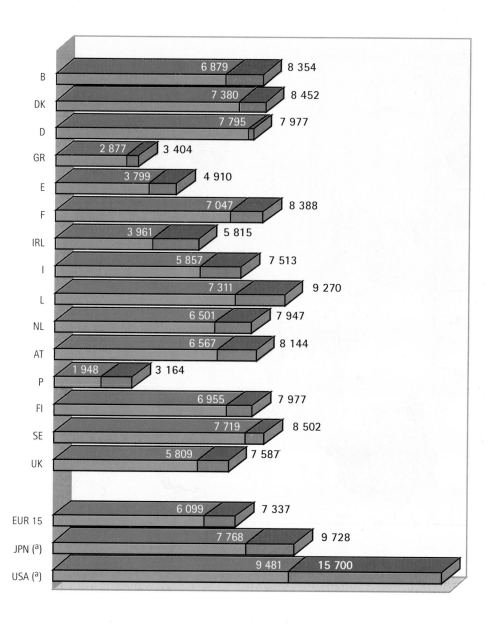

	6 879	8 354
B		
	7 380	8 452
DK		
	7 795	7 977
D		
GR	2 877	3 404
E	3 799	4 910
	7 047	8 388
F		
IRL	3 961	5 815
	5 857	7 513
I		
	7 311	9 270
L		
	6 501	7 947
NL		
	6 567	8 144
AT		
P	1 948	3 164
	6 955	7 977
FI		
	7 719	8 502
SE		
UK	5 809	7 587
	6 099	7 337
EUR 15		
	7 768	9 728
JPN (a)		
USA (a)	9 481	15 700

▨ 1982

▪ 1992   (a) 1979-1989.

Source: Eurostat.

Average annual variation of household consumption by volume percentage

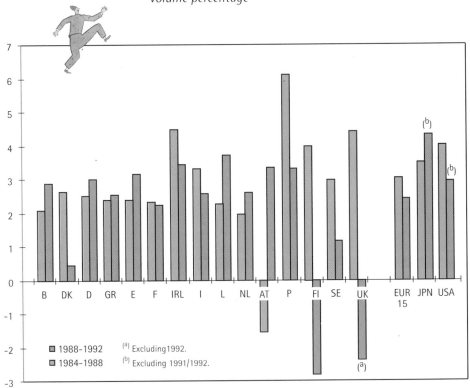

■ 1988-1992   (a) Excluding 1992.
■ 1984-1988   (b) Excluding 1991/1992.

Consumer spending: a more detailed picture
Categories as a percentage of total household consumption, 1992

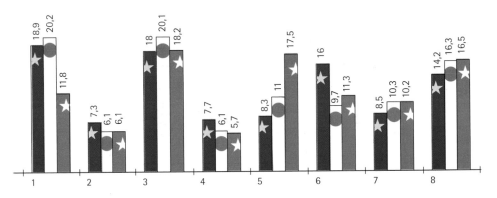

1 Food
2 Clothing
3 Housing, heating and lighting
4 Furniture and routine maintenance
5 Medical services and health
6 Transport and communications
7 Leisure, entertainment, education and culture
8 Other goods and services

Source: Eurostat.

Social security: wide variations between Member States
Social security expenditure as a percentage of gross domestic product (1993) [a]

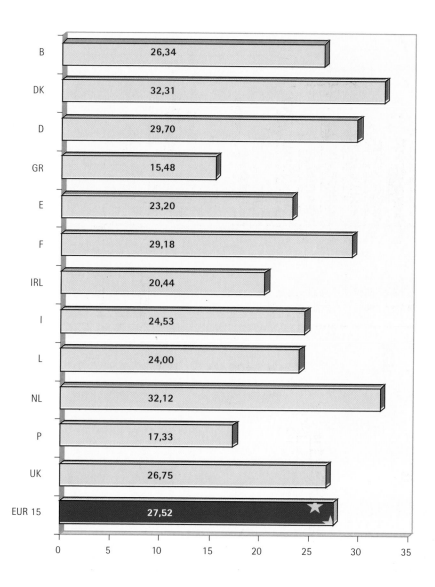

B	26,34
DK	32,31
D	29,70
GR	15,48
E	23,20
F	29,18
IRL	20,44
I	24,53
L	24,00
NL	32,12
P	17,33
UK	26,75
EUR 15	27,52

0   5   10   15   20   25   30   35

[a] Provisional figures, except for Denmark. Data not available for Austria, Finland and Sweden.

STANDARD OF LIVING

Source: Eurostat.

Private equipment: unevenly distributed

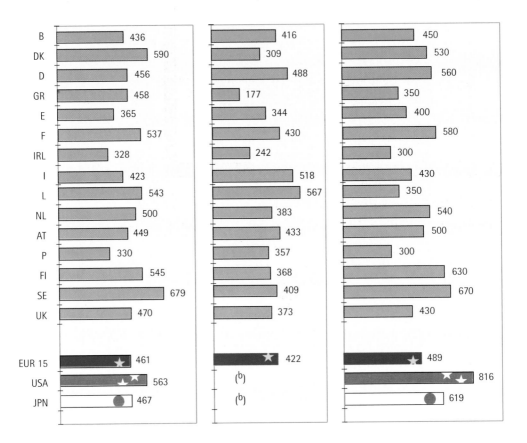

Telephones [a]
(per 1 000 persons, 1993)

Private cars
(per 1 000 persons, 1994)

Television sets
(per 1 000 persons, 1993)

	Telephones [a]	Private cars	Television sets
B	436	416	450
DK	590	309	530
D	456	488	560
GR	458	177	350
E	365	344	400
F	537	430	580
IRL	328	242	300
I	423	518	430
L	543	567	350
NL	500	383	540
AT	449	433	500
P	330	357	300
FI	545	368	630
SE	679	409	670
UK	470	373	430
EUR 15	461	422	489
USA	563	[b]	816
JPN	467	[b]	619

[a] Main line.
[b] Data not available.

Employment

Workforce and unemployment
Employment by sector

EMPLOYMENT

Source: Eurostat.

Jobs and unemployment: a priority

Working population as a percentage of the total population

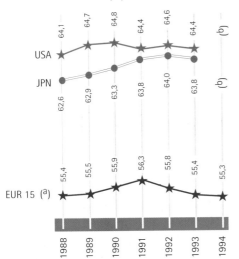

USA: 64,1 64,7 64,8 64,4 64,6 64,4 (b)

JPN: 62,6 62,9 63,3 63,8 64,0 63,8 (b)

EUR 15 (a): 55,4 55,5 55,9 56,3 55,8 55,4 55,3

1988 1989 1990 1991 1992 1993 1994

(a) Estimates.
(b) Data not available.

Unemployment as a percentage of the working population, in April each year

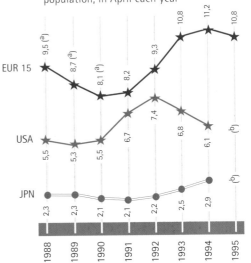

EUR 15: 9,5 (a) 8,7 (a) 8,1 (a) 8,2 9,3 10,8 11,2 10,8

USA: 5,5 5,3 5,5 6,7 7,4 6,8 6,1 (b)

JPN: 2,3 2,3 2,1 2,1 2,2 2,5 2,9 (b)

1988 1989 1990 1991 1992 1993 1994 1995

(a) EUR 12.
(b) Data not available.

Civilian working population (percentage, 1994)

(a) 1993.

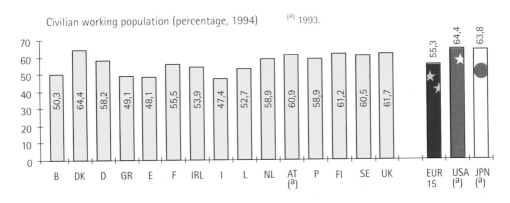

B	DK	D	GR	E	F	IRL	I	L	NL	AT (a)	P	FI	SE	UK	EUR 15	USA (a)	JPN (a)
50,3	64,4	58,2	49,1	48,1	55,5	53,9	47,4	52,7	58,9	60,9	58,9	61,2	60,5	61,7	55,3	64,4	63,8

Unemployment (percentage, 1995)

(a) 1994 average.   (b) Data not available.

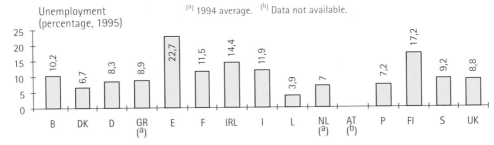

B	DK	D	GR (a)	E	F	IRL	I	L	NL (a)	AT (b)	P	FI	S	UK
10,2	6,7	8,3	8,9	22,7	11,5	14,4	11,9	3,9	7		7,2	17,2	9,2	8,8

Source: Eurostat.

Employment: breakdown between men and women
Civilian working population as a percentage of the total population (1994)

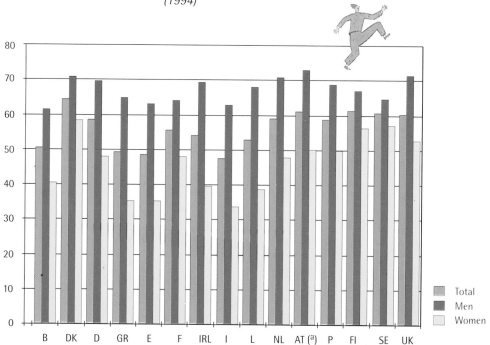

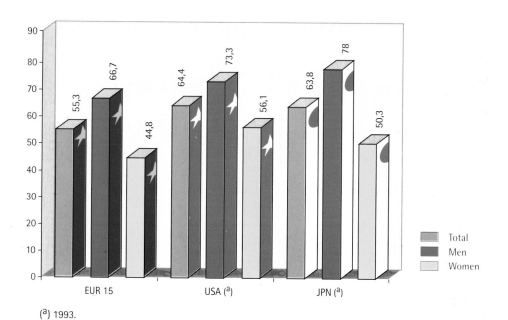

(a) 1993.

Source: Eurostat.

Unemployment: higher for women than for men
Unemployment rate by sex (percentage, 1995)

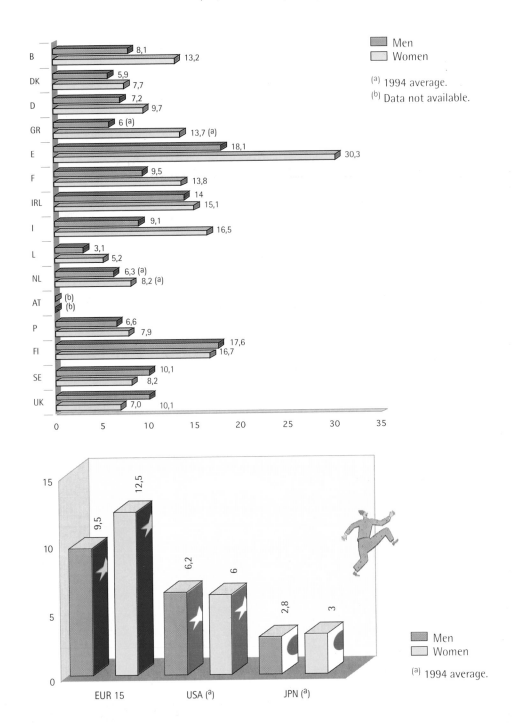

Men
Women

[a] 1994 average.
[b] Data not available.

	Men	Women
B	8,1	13,2
DK	5,9	7,7
D	7,2	9,7
GR	6 [a]	13,7 [a]
E	18,1	30,3
F	9,5	13,8
IRL	14	15,1
I	9,1	16,5
L	3,1	5,2
NL	6,3 [a]	8,2 [a]
AT	[b]	[b]
P	6,6	7,9
FI	17,6	16,7
SE	10,1	8,2
UK	7,0	10,1

Men
Women

[a] 1994 average.

	Men	Women
EUR 15	9,5	12,5
USA [a]	6,2	6
JPN [a]	2,8	3

Source: Eurostat.

Unemployment: the worst affected
Women (as a percentage of total unemployed, 1995)

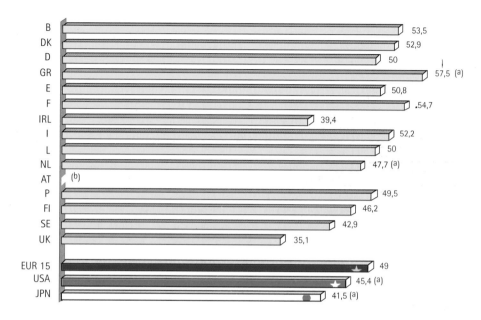

B	53,5
DK	52,9
D	50
GR	57,5 (a)
E	50,8
F	.54,7
IRL	39,4
I	52,2
L	50
NL	47,7 (a)
AT	(b)
P	49,5
FI	46,2
SE	42,9
UK	35,1
EUR 15	49
USA	45,4 (a)
JPN	41,5 (a)

(a)1994. (b) Data not available.

Unemployment: the worst affected
People under 25 (as a percentage, 1995)

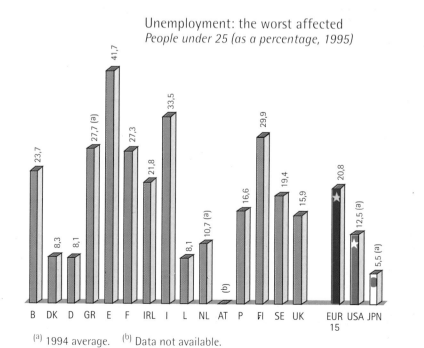

B	DK	D	GR	E	F	IRL	I	L	NL	AT	P	FI	SE	UK	EUR 15	USA	JPN
23,7	8,3	8,1	27,7 (a)	41,7	27,3	21,8	33,5	8,1	10,7 (a)	(b)	16,6	29,9	19,4	15,9	20,8	12,5 (a)	5,5 (a)

(a) 1994 average.   (b) Data not available.

Source: Eurostat.

Unemployment: marked regional disparities
*Unemployment rates in regions of the Union
(percentage, 1994)*

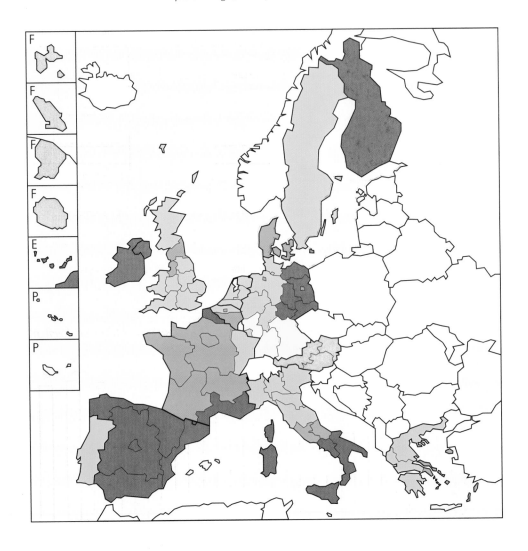

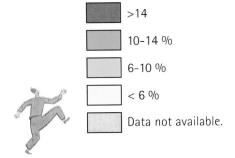

▨	>14
▨	10-14 %
▨	6-10 %
▢	< 6 %
▨	Data not available.

Source: Eurostat.

Employment sectors: the growth in services
Total employment by sector (percentage)

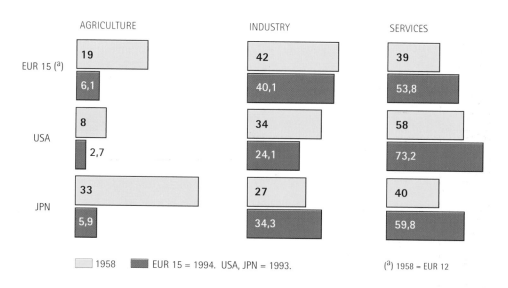

1958   EUR 15 = 1994. USA, JPN = 1993.   (ª) 1958 = EUR 12

Employment in services as a proportion of total employment (percentage, 1994)

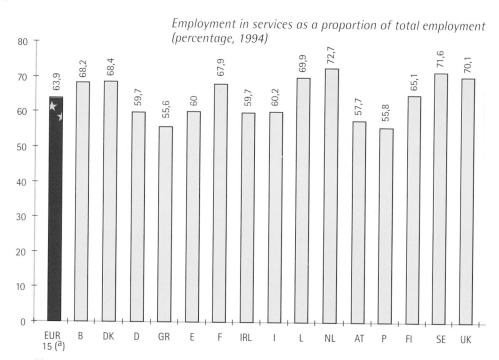

(ª) Calculated on a different basis from the previous table.

Economy

Services
Industry
Agriculture
Transport
Tourism
Energy supply
Inflation

Source: Eurostat.

Services dominant
The share of services in gross value-added (percentage, 1994)

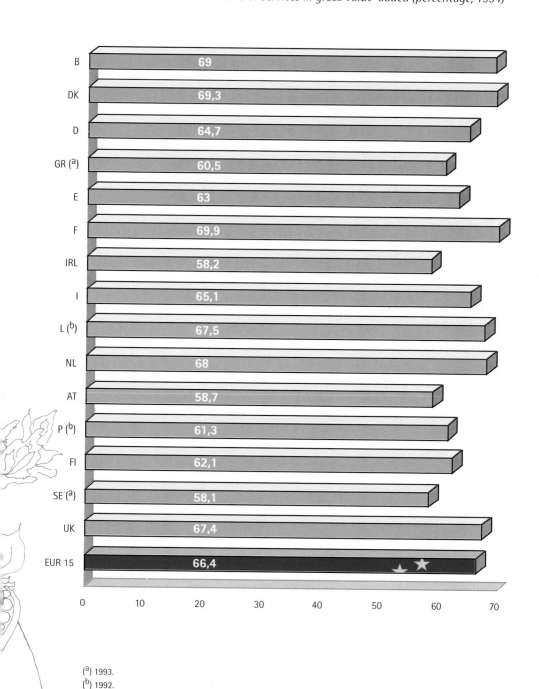

B	69
DK	69,3
D	64,7
GR (a)	60,5
E	63
F	69,9
IRL	58,2
I	65,1
L (b)	67,5
NL	68
AT	58,7
P (b)	61,3
FI	62,1
SE (a)	58,1
UK	67,4
EUR 15	66,4

0   10   20   30   40   50   60   70

(a) 1993.
(b) 1992.

Source: Eurostat.

Industry: the challenge facing Europe
Industrial production trends (1990 = 100)

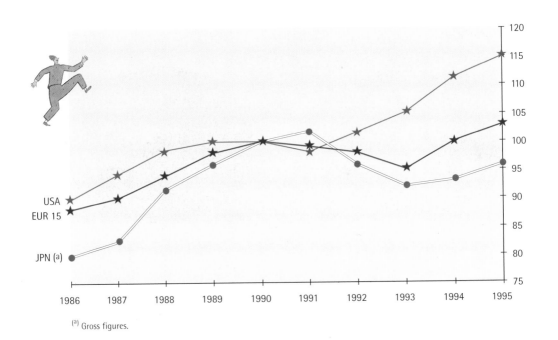

(a) Gross figures.

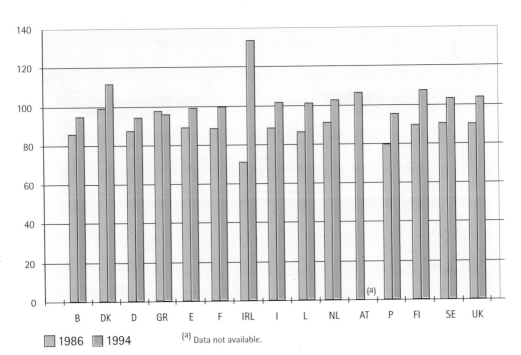

1986   1994

(a) Data not available.

Source: Eurostat.

European agriculture in the world: a major force
Share of world production (percentage, 1994)

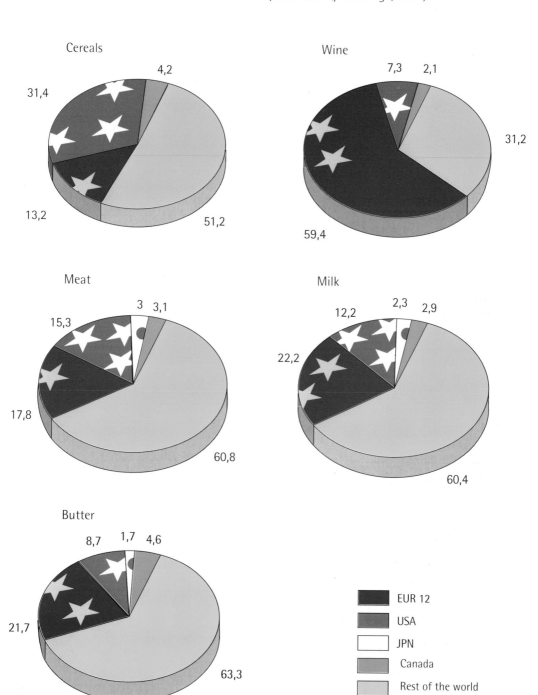

Cereals

4,2
31,4
13,2
51,2

Wine

7,3 2,1
31,2
59,4

Meat

3 3,1
15,3
17,8
60,8

Milk

2,3 2,9
12,2
22,2
60,4

Butter

8,7 1,7 4,6
21,7
63,3

■ EUR 12
■ USA
□ JPN
▨ Canada
▨ Rest of the world

Source: Eurostat.

Transport: highly developed networks
Roads (including motorways), km per 100 km², 1994

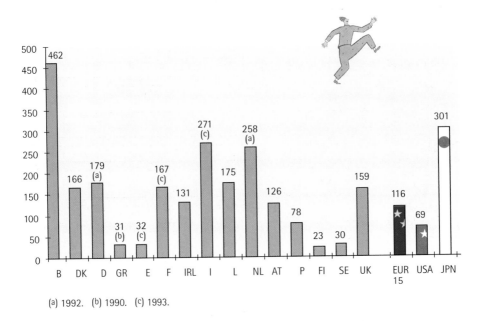

(a) 1992.   (b) 1990.   (c) 1993.

Motorways and railways, km per 1 000 km², 1994

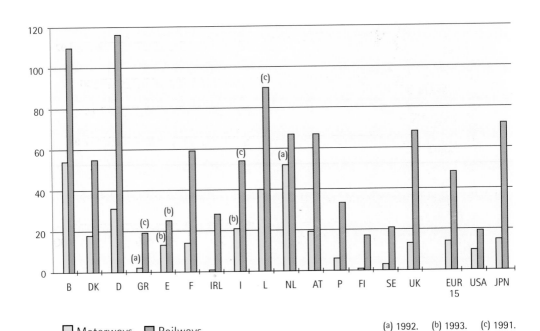

☐ Motorways   ■ Railways

(a) 1992.   (b) 1993.   (c) 1991.

Source: Eurostat.

Transport: vital for the single market
*Volume of freight by type of surface transport
(as a percentage of total, 1992)*

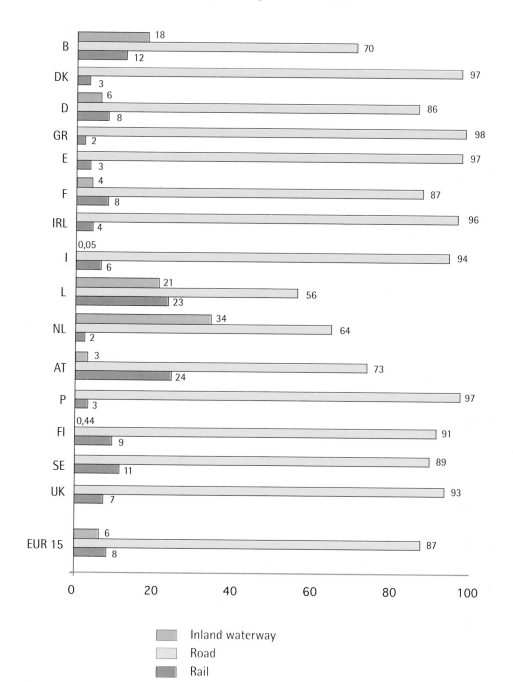

	Inland waterway
	Road
	Rail

Source: Eurostat.

Tourism: an important sector
To and from ... (revenue and expenditure in international tourism, million ECU, 1994)

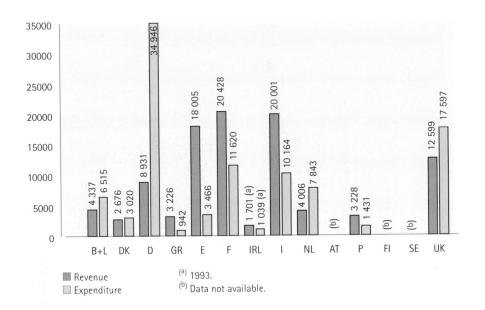

■ Revenue
☐ Expenditure

(a) 1993.
(b) Data not available.

Number of hotels and other establishments in 1994

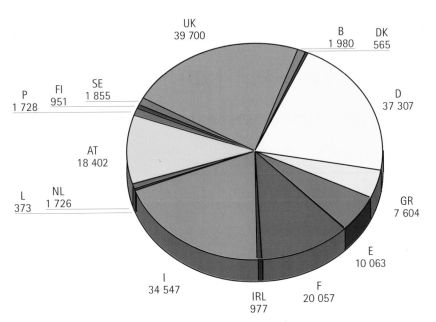

UK 39 700
B 1 980
DK 565
D 37 307
GR 7 604
E 10 063
F 20 057
IRL 977
I 34 547
NL 1 726
L 373
AT 18 402
P 1 728
FI 951
SE 1 855

EUR 15 = 177 835

Source: Eurostat.

Energy: Europe less dependent
Degree of energy dependence (percentage) [a]

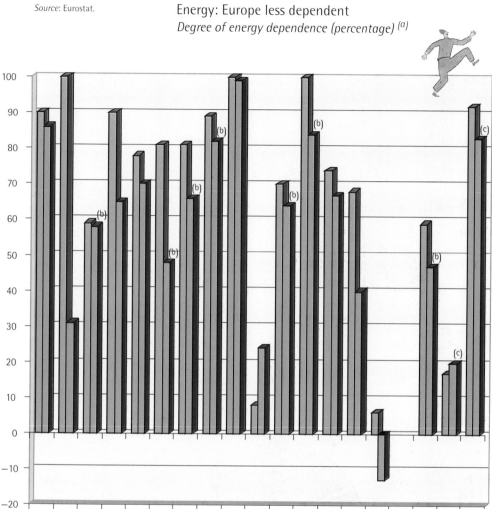

■ 1980

■ 1994

[a] Net imports (imports minus exports) as a proportion of total consumption.
[b] Provisional figure.
[c] 1993.

Source: Eurostat.

Has inflation been beaten?
Consumer price index: annual variation (percentage)

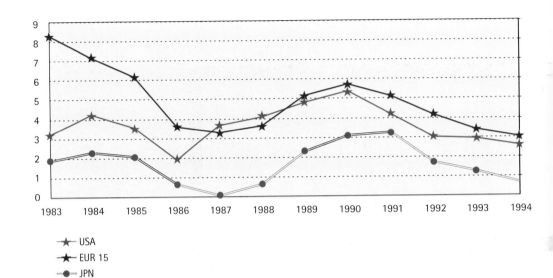

- ─★─ USA
- ─★─ EUR 15
- ─●─ JPN

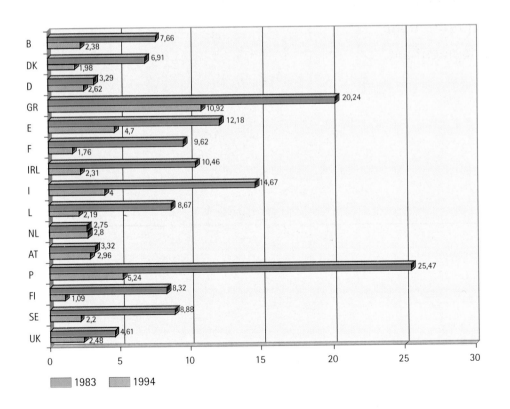

1983   1994

Europe in the world

International trade
Agricultural trade
Development aid

Source: Eurostat.

Trade: the world's biggest trading block partner
Breakdown of world trade (percentage, 1994)

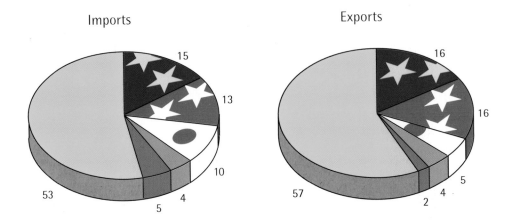

Imports
15
13
10
4
5
53

Exports
16
16
5
4
2
57

Agricultural trade: Europe, the world leader
*Shares of world trade in agricultural products
(percentage, 1994)*

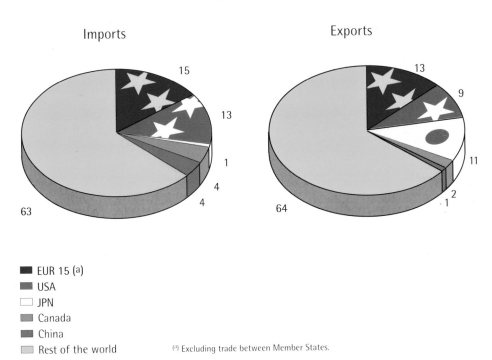

Imports
15
13
1
4
4
63

Exports
13
9
11
2
1
64

■ EUR 15 (a)
■ USA
□ JPN
■ Canada
■ China
■ Rest of the world

(a) Excluding trade between Member States.

Source: Eurostat.

Aid to the Third World: the European Union leads the way

Public aid from the principal donor countries (million dollars, 1992)

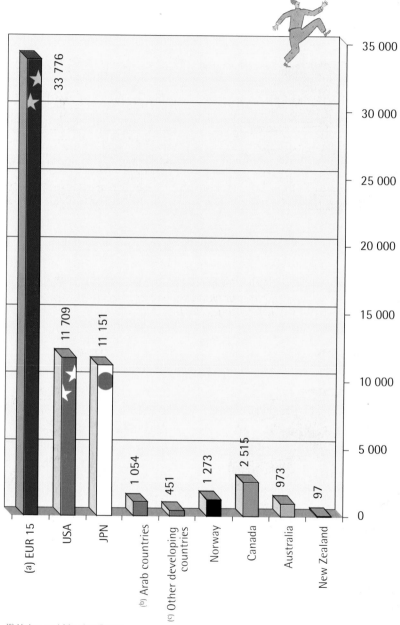

Country	Aid (million dollars)
(a) EUR 15	33 776
USA	11 709
JPN	11 151
(b) Arab countries	1 054
(c) Other developing countries	451
Norway	1 273
Canada	2 515
Australia	973
New Zealand	97

(a) Union and Member States.

(b) Including Saudi Arabia and United Arab Emirates.

(c) Including China, India, South Korea, Taiwan, Venezuela.

The European Union and its citizens

The Union budget
The European Parliament
Public opinion and Europe

Source: European Commission, DG XIX.

The European Union budget: limited expenditure

Breakdown of expenditure (as a percentage of the total)

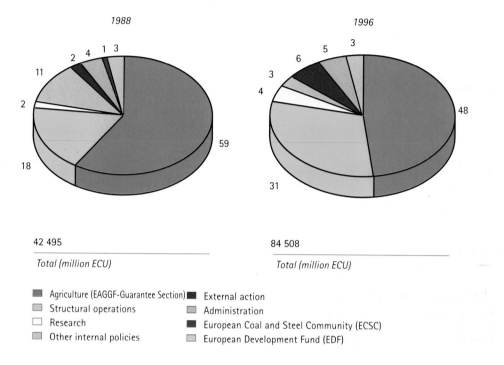

1988

2 4 1 3
11
2
18
59

1996

5 3
6
3
4
48
31

42 495

Total (million ECU)

84 508

Total (million ECU)

- ▦ Agriculture (EAGGF-Guarantee Section)
- ▦ Structural operations
- ▢ Research
- ▦ Other internal policies
- ■ External action
- ▦ Administration
- ■ European Coal and Steel Community (ECSC)
- ▦ European Development Fund (EDF)

Union expenditure as a percentage of Member States' GDP

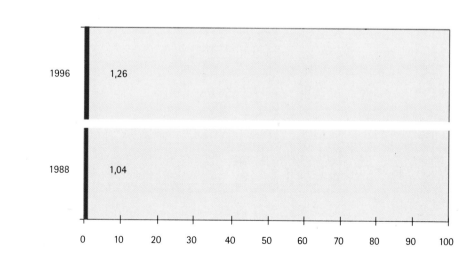

1996   1,26

1988   1,04

0   10   20   30   40   50   60   70   80   90   100

Source: European Parliament.

The European Parliament: the voice of the people
Distribution of seats by political group [a]

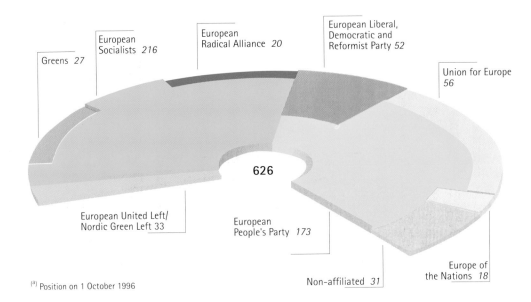

Greens *27*

European
Socialists *216*

European
Radical Alliance *20*

European Liberal,
Democratic and
Reformist Party *52*

Union for Europe
56

626

European United Left/
Nordic Green Left 33

European
People's Party *173*

Europe of
the Nations *18*

Non-affiliated *31*

[a] Position on 1 October 1996

Number of seats per country

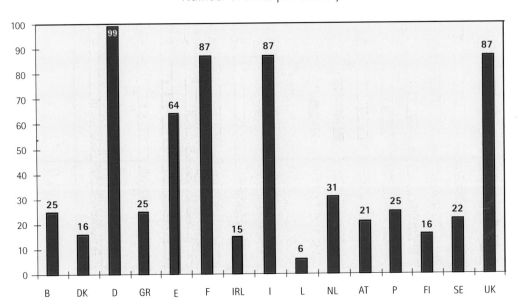

Public opinion and Europe

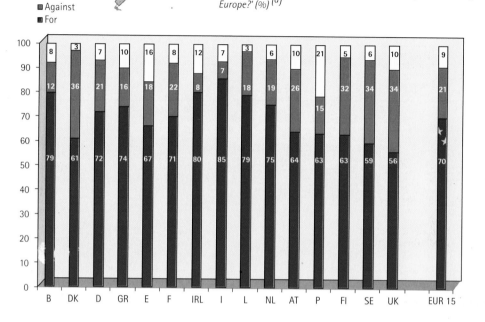

□ Don't know
■ Against
■ For

'In general, are you for or against the efforts being made to unify Europe?' (%) [a]

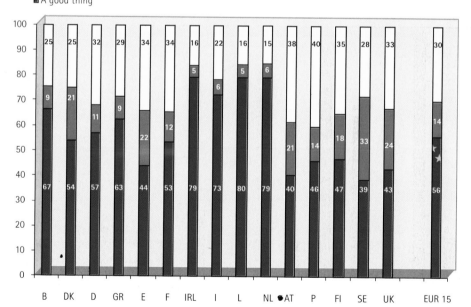

□ Neither good nor bad/don't know
■ A bad thing
■ A good thing

'Is your country's membership of the European Union a good or a bad thing?' (%) [a]

[a] Replies to Eurobarometer survey No 43, carried out for the European Commission by INRA (Europe). Some 16 000 people were questioned in May 1995.

European Commission
THE EUROPEAN UNION: KEY FIGURES
Luxembourg: Office for Official Publications of the
European Communities

1997 — 39 pp. — 16.2 x 22.9 cm

ISBN 92-827-7941-6

This booklet contains a series of charts on the population of the European Union and its Member States, their standard of living, employment, economy, Europe's place in the world, and the Union and its citizens. The charts, drawn up with the valuable help of Eurostat, the European Statistical Office, also show comparisons with the rest of the world and, in particular, with the Union's main partners and competitors.

EUROSTAT YEARBOOK '95 ◀

Straightforward and comprehensive, this publication is the essential reference work for anyone involved in Europe's economic and political affairs. It provides a detailed comparison of the major features of the Member States of the European Union and its main partners.
1995
489 pages
9 languages
30 ECU

▶ SOCIAL PORTRAIT OF EUROPE

Provides a view of the EU's social condition and offers an insight into the richness and diversity of the societies comprising the Union, as well as the complexity of the challenges that the social policies of the Union and its Member States are confronted with.
2nd edition - 1995
262 pages
DE-EN-FR
35 ECU

▼ WOMEN AND MEN IN THE EUROPEAN UNION

Compares the living conditions of men and women. The information which has been brought together in this publication reveals some surprising facts which will interest researchers, academics, special-interest groups, political decision-makers, trade unions and every man and woman in the EU or elsewhere.
1995
212 pages
DE-EN-FR
12 ECU

EUROPE IN FIGURES ▼

Sets out to provide accurate, independent and objective information on the progress of the European Union, its relations with the Member States and the rest of the world, its institutions and financing, as well as Community policies and the major statistical themes which Eurostat covers.
4th edition - 1995
425 pages
9 languages
15 ECU

BASIC STATISTICS OF THE EUROPEAN UNION ◀

This pocket-sized compilation provides the most important statistical data on the EU and comparison with several other European countries and the EU's major trading partners in the world. A handy and essential tool for providing quick information, this annual publication comes with colour graphs.
32nd edition - 1995
373 pages
9 languages
13 ECU

eurostat

EUROSTAT: Statistical Office of the European Communities

Data Shop Eurostat Luxembourg • 2, rue Jean Engling • L-1466 Luxembourg • tel: +352 4335 2251 • fax: +352 4335 22221
Data Shop Eurostat Bruxelles • 130, rue de la Loi • B-1049 Brussels • tel: +32-2 299 66 66 • fax: +32-2 295 01 25

The European Union: key figures

European
Commission

eurostat

COMMISSION OFFICES

Office in Ireland
39 Molesworth Street,
Dublin 2
Tel. 671 22 44

Office in England
Jean Monnet House,
8 Storey's Gate,
London SWIP 3AT
Tel. (171) 973 1992

Office in Wales
4 Cathedral Road,
Cardiff CF1 9SG
Tel. 37 16 31

Office in Scotland
9 Alva Street,
Edinburgh EH2 4PH
Tel. 225 20 58

Office in Northern Ireland
Windsor House,
9/15 Bedford Street,
Belfast BT2 7EG
Tel. 24 07 08

Information services in the USA
2100 M Street, NW,
Suite 707,
Washington DC 20037
Tel. (202) 862 95 00
305 East 47th Street,
3 Dag Hammarskjöld Plaza,
New York, NY 10017
Tel. (212) 371 38 04

Commission offices also exist in th
other countries of the European Ur
and in other parts of the world.

Growing from six Member States in 1952 to 15 by 1995, the European Union today embraces more than 370 million people, from the Arctic Circle to Portugal, from Ireland to Crete. Though rich in diversity, the Member States share certain common values. By entering into partnership together, their aim is to promote democracy, peace, prosperity and a fairer distribution of wealth.

This booklet contains a series of charts on the population of the Union and its Member States, their standard of living, employment, economy, Europe's place in the world, and the Union and its citizens. The charts, drawn up with the valuable help of Eurostat, the European Statistical Office, also show comparisons with the rest of the world and, in particular, with the Union's main partners and competitors.

OFFICE FOR OFFICIAL PUBLICATIONS
OF THE EUROPEAN COMMUNITIES
L-2985 Luxembourg

CM-97-96-798-EN-C

ISSN 1022-8233

ISBN 92-827-7941-6

9 789282 779415